Getting Started in PUNCH NEEDLE

Landauer Books

Copyright© 2006 by Landauer Corporation

This book was designed, produced, and published by Landauer Books
A division of Landauer Corporation
3100 NW 101st Street, Urbandale, IA 50322
www.landauercorp.com

President/Publisher: Jeramy Lanigan Landauer
Director of Operations: Kitty Jacobson
Editor in Chief: Becky Johnston
Project Editor: Connie McCall
Art Director: Linda Bender
Contributing Technical Advisor: Sue McAdoo
Graphic Design: Laurel Albright
Technical Writer: Rhonda Matus
Technical Illustrator: Linda Bender
Editorial Assistant: Debby Burgraff
Photographer: Craig Anderson Photography
We also wish to thank punch needle specialists Kristan DiBiase, Laura DiBiase, Charlotte Dudney,
Karen Gates, Marilyn Lopez, April Mathis, Sue McAdoo, Linda Repasky, Helen Stetina and Sally Van Nuys.

Library of Congress Cataloging-in-Publication Data

Getting started in punch needle/[editor-in-chief, Becky Johnston].
    p. com.
  ISBN-13: 978-0-9770166-5-5
  ISBN-10: 0-9770166-5-X
  1. Canvas embroidery–Patterns. 2. Miniature quilts. 3. Miniature craft. I. Johnston, Becky.

TT778.C3G32 2006
746.44'2041–dc22

2005057921

ISBN 10:   0-9770166-5-X
ISBN 13: 978-0-9770166-5-5

This book printed on acid-free paper.
Printed in USA
10-9-8-7-6-5-4-3-2-1

Punch Needle Miniature Album Quilt

The punch needle miniature album quilt featured in this book (shown above) is inspired by a circa 1840 Maryland Album appliqué quilt that is now in the permanent collection of the Shelburne Museum in Shelburne, Vermont. The original bed-size *Horse and Birds Album Quilt,* which measures an impressive 98" x 101", has been replicated in punch needle through the use of 25 blocks scaled to 5" each, with borders added to make a quilt that measures a mere 30" x 30". Individual blocks are suitable for framing, or the miniature masterpiece quilt may be displayed as a welcoming wallhanging.

FOREWORD

Welcome to the world of punch needle embroidery! This book is a beautiful introduction to the needlework technique that has been a passion of mine for nearly 30 years. When I started, there were no detailed books like this to follow. In 1979, I did write a book with basic designs and instructions for Dover Press—*Russian Punchneedle Embroidery*—which is still in print.

Although there were no published books at the time, there were enthusiastic artists who were developing ways to use punch needles beyond the ways of the Old Believers, the Russian immigrants to the United States who brought with them their punch needle embroidery. The Old Believers' use of the technique was limited to punching with a single strand of thread and strictly following the weave of the fabric rather than the shape of the design. They added colorful designs, using a verys short pile punched with a single thread, for floral motifs of exquisite detail on their rubashkas (men's shirts), rukavas (women's blouses), festive aprons, and decorative cloths that framed the icons prominent in their living quarters. Their word for this fine embroidery is *igolochkoy*, meaning "with a little needle," for the technique and its product. It is also my trade-marked name (Igolochkoy™) for punch needles that the Old Believers were instrumental in developing and hand-crafting in the late 1960s.

Early artists, especially Jean Cook, Marinda Brown (Stewart), Mary Manocchio, Linda Nakashima, and Barbara Michelsen, went beyond the single thread and low pile designs to create more texture by using larger punch needles. DMC thread was available in a wide variety of colors (important for good design) and came as six threads twisted together (floss). The twisted threads of the floss could be easily separated, and as a result, the 2 to 3-strand and 4, 5, or 6-strand punch needles were developed. This led to artists combining thread colors and different types of threads, and using a broad variety of woven fabrics. Larger designs were now more practical with larger needles. Today, there are punch needle enthusiasts who create miniatures (such as rugs to scale for doll houses), cloth dolls, clothing embellishments, fashion accessories (purses, belts, necklaces), and quilts (crazy quilts, pictorial quilts, landscape quilts, and quilted wearable art).

Quilters using the punch needle technique began showing their work about 20 years ago at the International Quilt Market in Houston, Texas. Judith Montano used it in her crazy quilting as an additional embroidery stitch and on her fashions for the famous Houston Fashion Show. Carol Lane Saber, Linda Nakashima, and Marinda Stewart also exhibited elaborate garments using metallic, silk, and ribbon threads in punch needle designs that were spectacular. Their use of the technique to embellish garments is in the tradition of the Old Believers but it is done with a greater versatility of design.

About three years ago, Linda Repasky exhibited in Vermont with her own original rugs (hooked) and an identical miniature rug (punched) beside it, which caught the attention of many rug hookers. Artists like Missy Stevens produce thread "paintings" with punch needle and are able to command high prices for their work. While teaching in Pennsylvania recently, I met an elderly gentleman who produced a king-size Baltimore Album quilt in punch needle (a monumental achievement). There are many more quilters, famous or not-so-famous, that love to use punch needle embroidery in their projects.

Each of the punch needle specialists who contributed to this book deserves a round of applause for helping to bring this art form into the mainstream of needlework. This book highlights their accomplishments and provides a unique approach to learning the basics of punch needle embroidery.

By punching each block adapted from the circa 1840 *Horse and Birds Album Quilt* from the collection of Shelburne Museum, Shelburne, Vermont, you will become "hooked" on this simple, fast, and beautiful technique. As a beginner working with just a few colors, after a little practice you will become a pro. If you have previously done some punching or a lot of punching, you'll pick up some new techniques and new products on the market. Regardless of your skill level, don't be afraid to "break the rules" regarding color of thread, fabric background, size of needle, length of loop you punch, etc. For example, compare the original appliqué pineapple design of the historic quilt to the punch needle rendition. Note that the original body of the pineapple was a single-color fabric with quilting stitches offering the suggestion of a pineapple surface. The punched version uses different thread colors and pile heights to visually achieve a pineapple surface.

The horizon before you is unlimited as you embark on this wonderful adventure of adding texture to a woven fabric. The heirloom that you create using these 22 designs will be cherished by future generations. Be sure to sign and date any of your finished work.

Gail Bird
Owner, Birdhouse Enterprises

Contents

Contents

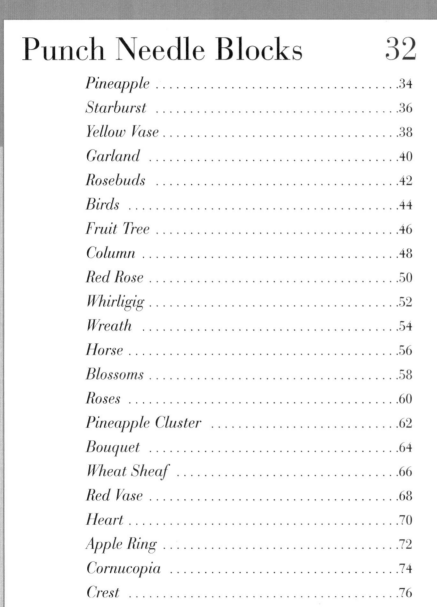

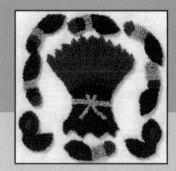

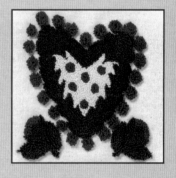

INTRODUCTION

Punch needle embroidery, commonly known as Russian punch needle (translated from the word Igolochkoy meaning it is done "with a little needle"), is a time-honored form of needlework that is enjoying widespread renewal. And why not? Punch needle embroidery is an appealing art form, rich in color and texture, which works up quickly using a few simple tools and materials.

A brief history

The ancient Egyptians were among the first to develop and use the punch needle technique. During the Middle Ages, a form of punch needle was widely used in Europe, especially to decorate ecclesiastical clothing and specialized items for the church. In modern times, the art has been associated with embroidery done by Russian immigrants, members of a sect called the Old Believers. Both the ancient Egyptians and the Russian Old Believers made needles from the hollow bones of birds' wings. Today's punch needle tools have been vastly improved!

Themes in punch needle

Because of its historical roots, punch needle often incorporates familiar symbols and folk art images in the design motifs, images such as fruit, flowers, birds and animals. The pineapple, a symbol of hospitality, has been a familiar and enduring element in American quilt and punch needle designs for generations.

In 1493, Christopher Columbus returned from his second voyage to the Caribbean, bringing to Europe a pineapple cultivated on the island of Guadeloupe. The fruit was virtually unknown in Europe, and its exotic nature and sweetness took the continent by storm.

For 200 years European horticulturists tried to find a way to grow pineapples in a hothouse. In the mid-1500s, Spanish and Portuguese ships took the fruit to India, where it took hold beautifully. The pineapple kept increasing in popularity and importance, becoming such a coveted delight that it was an appropriate gift to present to a king.

In America, the pineapple became closely associated with the hospitality that was the center of Colonial social life. It is said that after a voyage, ship captains would put a pineapple on the porch railing as a way of saying that they were home and would welcome company.

Visitors were everywhere highly valued, and the pineapple symbolized the warmest welcome a hostess could extend to her guests. A pineapple was often placed in the center of the dining table; in a family of some means, the pineapple might serve as dessert. Colonial grocers actually rented pineapples to hostesses whose limited means did not allow for such an expensive purchase; the pineapple was returned and then sold to a wealthier customer.

The pineapple motif was also used in home furnishings. Bed posts were topped by carved pineapples, and the familiar image appeared in many other kinds of household décor and linens.

Basics of punch needle

Getting started in punch needle is as easy as purchasing an inexpensive embroidery hoop, a punch needle, a few skeins of embroidery floss and a piece of weaver's cloth. Embroidery floss is passed through the length of a slender, hollow "little needle." The design is punched onto cloth that is stretched drum-tight over an embroidery hoop. The punching is done from the back, leaving closely placed loops of floss on the front, a process that can be described as rug-hooking-in-reverse. Because punch needle motifs are created with just a few strands of embroidery floss, most punch needle designs are small, less than 6 inches across and sometimes only an inch or two in size. The designs lend themselves to small, elegant embellishments for clothing and accessories or for home décor.

Quilts in miniature

Working similar designs as individual blocks and then combining the blocks into a miniature quilt produces dramatic results. The 22 motifs featured on the following pages are inspired by the impressive circa 1840 *Horse and Birds Album Quilt* from Shelburne Museum, Shelburne, Vermont. The punch needle motifs are first worked as 5-inch blocks and then pieced together and quilted to create a one-of-a-kind miniature punch needle quilt. As in the original quilt, the pineapple symbol of hospitality is repeated in the four corner blocks of the miniature replica.

Whether you choose to make one or all of the 22 charming motifs offered in this collection, we invite you to discover for yourself the joys of getting started in punch needle embroidery.

Horse and Birds Album Quilt

The *Horse and Birds Album Quilt* is in the permanent collection of Shelburne Museum, Shelburne, Vermont. The quilt was probably made around 1840 by a member of the Hundloser family. Like many quilts of the era, it was sold during the Civil War to raise money, in this case for the Confederate Army. The quilt, which measures 98" x 101", is pieced and appliquéd in plain and printed cotton fabrics. The quilting is in a palm design for the background and also forms the white flowers. A ribbon indicates that the quilt won "First Premium" distinction in the Household division at the Maryland State Fair in 1939. Shelburne Museum founder Electra Havemeyer Webb purchased the quilt for presentation to the museum.

ALBUM QUILTS

The years from 1825 to 1850—the second quarter of the nineteenth century—were packed with expansion and invention in virtually every aspect of American culture. These advancements contributed to a remarkable surge in the making of quilts. The Album quilt was part of that surge.

In terms of geographical expansion, "Westward Ho!" was the motto of the thousands of Americans who moved westward to settle the Mississippi Valley, the Midwest, the Great Plains, Texas, and even California. Quilts were given to families as practical comforts and as reminders of home, and quilts also were made along the way.

Technology had produced the steel plow and the reaper, making it possible for those settlers to break up the sod of the Western grasslands and grow grain. Factory-based mass production made all sorts of other goods and tools available to ordinary people. This was especially true of fabric production; millions of yards of factory-woven,

roller-printed fabric became available for bedding, clothing, and of course quilt-making.

Especially in city homes, new stoves and steam radiators warmed daily life. New types of lamps made it easy for a woman to spend an evening reading *Godey's Lady's Book* or other women's publications with their stories, poems, homemaking advice, fashion information, and quilt patterns.

Curiously, it was one tiny piece of all this cultural change—the autograph book—that fostered a new quilt form, the Friendship or Album quilt.

Autograph books were wildly popular by 1825, with many homes displaying one on a parlor table for visitors to sign. Women's magazines of the 1830s printed suitable sentimental poems and sayings. The 1840s were especially characterized by sentimentality, probably because of the waves of westward migration and widespread religious awakenings. This is the era of the Maryland Album quilt.

The Album quilt

Album quilts, which are notable for their beauty and refinement, originated at a time when the American middle class had a growing appreciation for a gentility akin to that of upper-class Europeans and Americans.

Typically, an Album quilt is composed of anywhere from 25 to 40 blocks, each block made by a different person. The blocks were then made into a quilt, often a gift presented to an honored recipient. Although some Album quilts have pieced blocks, most were appliquéd, often with motifs such as birds or flowers cut from chintz.

Many Album quilts were pictorial, showing familiar buildings or events that were meaningful to the potential owner. The individual blocks could be personal, for instance a picture of the person's home or farm; historical, for example a monument or patriotic emblems; themed, perhaps along musical or military lines, or just beautiful, with designs of flowers and fruits.

Album or Friendship quilts were usually made by a group, for some special event or occasion. Often finished blocks were arranged and sewn into a quilt at an Album party. Many of them were autographed by hand or by use of a metal signature-stamp. There were several popular types or uses of Album quilts.

Presentation Quilts, which were also called Friendship Quilts, typically were gifts for a favorite teacher, minister, or minister's wife, or for a doctor from his grateful patients. Each block might be signed and dated by its maker. Such quilts were often going-away gifts when the recipient was moving to a new job in another town, or moving west to resettle. Freedom quilts and Bride's quilts were often made and frequently autographed by family members and friends of the young person who would be honored.

The Freedom quilt

offers interesting insight into the daily life of that era. A Freedom quilt was given to a young man on his twenty-first birthday, when he completed his apprenticeship. In those days, young men were under legal obligation to their fathers or guardians, who could take their wages or make them work without pay. Contracts for apprenticeship specified many strong limitations on a young man; not only was he not to steal the master's goods or trade secrets, but he could not play certain unlawful games or, according to one contract, "haunt alehouses or playhouses." He could not marry during his apprenticeship. Hence, the Freedom Quilt was an appropriate congratulatory gift. The young man often kept the quilt to be given to his future bride.

The Bride's quilt

was carefully designed and meticulously made, sometimes entirely in white. If it was an Album quilt, it might show her new home or scenes from her childhood, or it might have elaborate sentimental designs of hearts and lovebirds. Sometimes the bride designed and made the quilt top, and others quilted it for her; sometimes it was designed by the older women who also quilted the dozen or so quilt tops that the young woman had made and stored in her dowry chest.

Not all Album quilts were products of collaboration. Some were made by individuals, as is clearly indicated by their uniformity of style. The quiltmaker might gather material from friends or family, getting enough material from each to make a complete block, and then she would make the blocks, assemble the quilt attractively, and have each friend sign the block for which she contributed the material.

The Baltimore Album quilt

As time went on, a particular form of Album quilt—and the best known—experienced almost a "fad" status for about a decade, roughly from 1845 to 1855. This is the Baltimore Album quilt, which is almost always appliquéd. Blocks vary in construction; some are just one thickness of appliqué, some are layered. Some are embellished with embroidery or inked drawings. The Baltimore Album quilts include some of the most beautiful quilts on record.

At least two of Baltimore's ethnic groups, the Germans and the English, contributed to the intricacy of Baltimore Album designs by using techniques familiar to them. Quilters among the German-Americans used the challenging scissors-and-paper art form known as Scherenschnitte, cutting intricate patterns out of paper and then using the patterns to cut cloth for

appliqué. The English-Americans used *broderie perse* (French for "Persian embroidery"), in which very close buttonhole stitching is used to appliqué pieces of chintz fabric to a background cloth. Note that at that time, "chintz" referred to very expensive floral prints imported from India.

Many blocks have a myriad of tiny pieces of brand new fabric, as opposed to pieces of recycled old clothing. Sometimes there are dozens of different fabrics in one block. Experts believe this evidence points to the Baltimore Album quilts' being made by persons of some means, probably the families of middle-class merchants.

Who designed these quilts? There were apparently at least three talented designers in Baltimore who may have had businesses providing patterns or kits for creating the fancier blocks. Some quilts are entirely based on these "professional" patterns, while others have them in the center with simpler designs in the outer portions. The quilters themselves were women of all ages, but research from dated quilts and population records suggests that women in their twenties predominated.

Because most of the Album quilts were used decoratively, unlike the utility quilts that endured years of wear and tear, many of these artistic historical treasures have survived the centuries and have been carefully preserved in museum collections for the inspiration and enjoyment of future generations of quilt lovers.

BASICS

Getting Started

Here and on the following pages, discover how easy it is to learn the art of punch needle. From fabric and floss to hoop and needle, you'll find everything you need to create your own punch needle masterpieces.

The fabric

In traditional embroidery, the fabric used for the background can vary from the sheerest silk to heaviest canvas. Fabric density is determined by the size of the threads used for weaving and how tightly those threads are woven together. However, the standard fabric used for punch needle embroidery is a medium-weight blend called weaver's cloth. It is a durable and washable fabric in a 50 percent cotton, 50 percent polyester blend. The blend produces a tight, firm weave that holds its shape well—a necessity for successful punch needle.

Weaver's cloth comes in white, natural, and khaki; it can have a lightly flecked appearance that makes it popular for use in country-style home furnishings such as kettle cloth kitchen curtains. It is sold by the piece or by the yard.

The thread or ribbon

Punch needle embroidery is a versatile art because the loops can be small, medium or large, depending on the size of the needle and the weight of the thread, ribbon or floss you use. Fine sewing or quilting thread such as the 100% Egyptian cotton, 50 weight Thimbleberries® collection by Robison-Anton Textile Company (shown below), is wound on a spool and is easy to use because it eliminates much of the tedious rethreading of the needle. Sewing or quilting thread works well for a tightly woven design reminiscent of the intricate detail of Russian punch needle.

Silk ribbon used for punch needle embroidery works up quickly because the loops are larger and the width of the ribbon easily fills the design area, requiring fewer punches. The finished look of the design motifs will be softer.

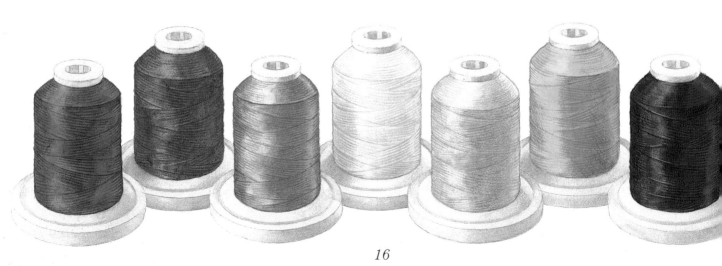

The floss

Cotton embroidery floss is inexpensive, easy to use, washable and available in a myriad of colors, making it ideal for punch needle embroidery. Embroidery floss is customarily packaged as a skein consisting of several-yards length of six-stranded thread bundled in a paper wrapper. The six-stranded thread can be easily separated and recombined in the number of strands the punch needle project requires. Most punch needle uses two or three strands of floss in a medium-sized needle. However, you can punch fine details with just one strand, using a smaller needle, or larger areas in six strands, using a larger needle. The designs in this book are based primarily on three-strand punching, with a few optional uses of just one strand.

Floss comes in hundreds of colors and shades, some vat-dyed in solid colors and some hand-dyed in color-on-color. DMC embroidery floss (shown below) is an example of vat-dyed floss. Its 8.7-yard skeins are available in hundreds of solid colors and in metallic finishes. The floss is 100 percent cotton and is both washable and colorfast. Anchor Thread also makes this kind of floss, though in fewer colors. Both manufacturers sell their floss primarily by color number.

Another kind of floss is hand-dyed in a technique called overdyeing. Like vat-dyed floss, overdyed floss is 100 percent cotton; however the dyes are not colorfast and therefore not suited for use on garments or home furnishings that will need to be washed from time to time. Experienced punch needle specialists use overdyed floss for many special effects, including an antique appearance. If you choose to use overdyed floss, buy enough from the same dye lot to finish your project. Weeks Dye Works produces hand-dyed, overdyed floss in dozens of colors, with 5 yards of six-strand floss in each skein. Sampler Threads™ from The Gentle Art is another floss that is hand-dyed and overdyed to give floss an antique look; it is usually cut in one-yard lengths.

All these and other companies also make other types of cotton thread, such as pearl cotton #8, that are suitable for punch needle. However, for the motifs in the 25 blocks in the punch needle miniature Album quilt featured in this book, yardage amounts and color numbers are given for using three strands of colorfast 100 percent cotton embroidery floss from Anchor or DMC. The color numbers are accompanied by an unofficial description of DMC colors often used in color charts.

The hoop or frame

Punch needle embroidery works best with a hoop or frame that is designed to allow you to stretch the weaver's cloth to the tightness that punch needle work requires—drum-tight.

The inexpensive Susan Bates® hoops are designed especially for punch needle use. These hoops come in several sizes, in round and oval shapes, and with a plain finish or in bright colors. The feature that makes Susan Bates hoops so well suited for punch needle work is their "Super-Grip Lip," an extra edge that holds the fabric extra tight, as is required for punch needle.

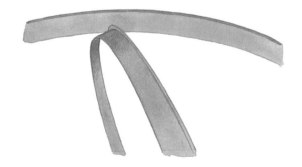

Similarly, another brand, the "No-Slip Hoop," has a tongue and groove feature around the perimeter of the hoop.

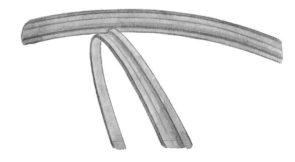

All of the hoops are equipped with thumb-screws for tightening. A rubberized jar gripper from any store that sells kitchenware will help you keep turning the thumb-screw to achieve adequate tightness.

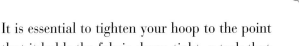

It is essential to tighten your hoop to the point that it holds the fabric drum-tight, a task that some punchers find very difficult and that may cause sore fingers. A tool that makes the job easier is the Perfect Hoop Screw developed by Pamela Gurney, an Australian punch needle artist who specializes in punching with silk ribbon (www.punchneedleembroidery.com).

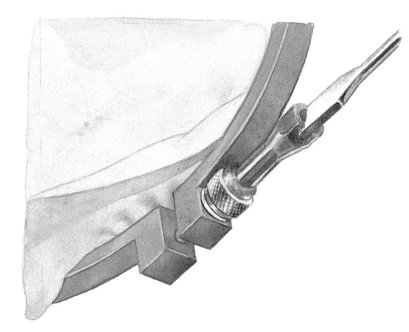

The Perfect Hoop Screw, of hand-crafted brass, replaces the hoop's existing thumb-screw, making hand-tightening easier. You can also tighten the hoop by using a coin or a screwdriver inserted in the slot at the end. Using the hoop screw also avoids making fabric marks with your thumb during tightening.

A recent innovation in frames for punch needle is a lap stand with carding strips, which are little metal gripping fingers that extend along the sides all the way to the corners. These carding strips are quite effective in securely holding the weaver's cloth in place.

The lap stand is a different approach to the hoop. It has a smaller and a larger hoop, connected by peg "legs" so you can work on either hoop and have the other one serve as a base in your lap. This leaves both hands free. Or, you can have two projects going, one on each hoop. The lap stand is collapsible and has the tongue and groove feature for tightness. One brand is the Morgan lap stand; another is Jennoop. Both kinds can be taken apart for storage or travel.

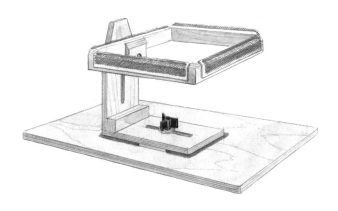

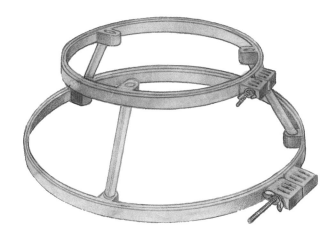

The needle & threader

The traditional Russian punch needle is a slender, hollow shaft. One side of the sharp pointed end is beveled; that is where the eye of the needle is. The thread runs through the length of the needle. These Russian Igolochkoy™ needles come in sets of three sizes, for use with one strand, three strands, or all six strands of embroidery floss.

shown actual size

CTR Needleworks makes the same three needle sizes (each sold separately) of the traditional punch needle, but with several features that make the needle easier to use. It is a little larger and thicker, so it is easier on the hands. Its punching tip has a little silver insert to make the beveled side easier to keep track of, helping you keep the needle in the correct position.

shown actual size

A little larger yet is the needle designed for punching with narrow silk ribbon. The needle is longer, and the tip is larger. Because the tip is larger, the punching motion is a little different. You punch by gently twisting the length of the needle through the fabric, fully up to the handle, allowing the tip to glide through an opening in the fabric. You need to hold the new loop of ribbon with your other hand, to keep the loop from slipping back up. The length of the needle (depth of the loop) is adjusted by means of a nut on the needle, sliding the shaft to set the desired depth.

With any punch needle, many users like to add a pencil grip (sold in stationery departments) to make it easier to hold onto for a length of time.

One essential tool required for use with any punch needle is a needle threader, which is made of very thin, stiff wires. The threader is inserted into the needle, the floss is inserted into the threader, and the threader then pulls the thread back through the needle. Threaders ordinarily come with the purchase of the needles, but they can be ordered separately.

shown actual size

The scissors

A pair of small, sharp-pointed and curved-blade embroidery scissors is a necessity for snipping stray floss ends without accidentally snipping off loops. Embroidery scissors come in several sizes and in a variety of designs, shapes, finishes, and of course prices. There are specialized models for just the left hand or just the right hand, and there are models that can be used in either hand.

The important thing to keep in mind is that your scissors have fine, sharp points and slim, curved blades. Double-curved scissors are especially helpful; they allow you to reach over the edge of the embroidery hoop while keeping your hand out of the way. A major scissors manufacturer is Gingher, which makes several models, some plain, some fancy, 3-1/2" or 4" in length.

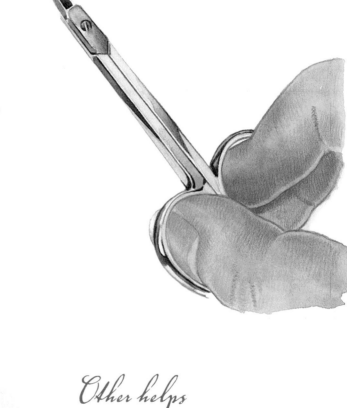

Other helps

There are many needle cases, floss organizers, and storage boxes made specifically for needlework use. Minimally, it is a good idea to have a transparent plastic lidded box that is large enough to hold your equipment and project. Place a magnetic strip into it to keep pins and threaders in place.

A wide array of small frames and boxes are available for displaying finished punch needle. Many of the design motifs adapted from the *Horse and Birds Album Quilt* that are featured in the miniature punch needle quilt blocks have a contemporary look and appeal. Design motifs such as the Pineapple and the Heart (shown at left) are suitable for framing.

Transferring the pattern

Use a transferring pencil, a black scrapbooking pen, a blue sewing pen, or some other fine-tipped, non-bleeding instrument to transfer the pattern to the fabric. Permanent pens and graphite pencils are not recommended because they do not permit making minor adjustments as you punch; the lines would still show.

To transfer the pattern to the fabric, first use a copier to make a copy of each of the full-size patterns that you plan to use (see Patterns, beginning on page 79). These patterns have already been reversed left to right and are ready to use.

If you have access to a light table, lay the paper pattern on the light table, lay the cloth over it, and carefully trace the pattern. You will not punch the lines of the box that appears around the pattern, but use the box to help you line up the design on the straight grain of the fabric.

If you do not have access to a light table, tape the paper pattern to a window that has good light coming through it, tape the cloth over the paper, and trace the pattern.

Loading the hoop

The hoop has two parts; the inner one has an extra lip on its edge, and outer one has the thumbscrew. Lay the inner hoop on the table, lip side up, and lay the fabric over it with the design facing up and centered in the hoop. Loosen the screw on the outer hoop. Lay the outer hoop over the inner hoop and fabric, making sure it pops down over the fabric. The extra lip locks the fabric so you can stretch it.

Begin to secure the fabric, tightening the thumbscrew. Pull the fabric down evenly all around, and tighten the hoop some more. Continue to work around the hoop, using your hand and your fingers to pull down firmly and evenly on the fabric, periodically tightening the hoop some more.

When the fabric is stretched tightly enough, it should sound a little like a snare drum when you tap it. Using a plastic jar gripper will help you tighten the thumbscrew. The rule is, "When you think it is tight, tighten it some more!" The hoop might become slightly distorted. Note that a person who has arthritic fingers may need help with the tightening process.

Threading the needle

Hold the wire needle-threader between the thumb and middle finger of your right hand. Holding the needle in your left hand, insert the twisted end of the wire needle-threader through the tip of the needle and out the end of the handle.

Pull the threader back through the tip of the needle, bringing the three strands of floss along with it until the floss extends several inches beyond the tip of the needle.

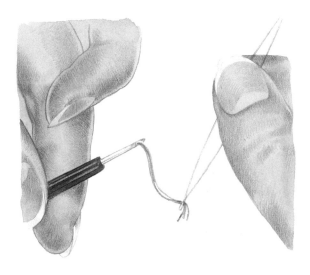

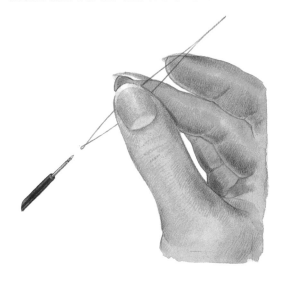

With the floss still in the loop of the threader, insert the other end of the threader into the eye of the needle. Use the threader to pull the floss through the eye of the needle, from the bevel side. Carefully remove the floss from the threader, and put the threader in a secure place (threaders are almost impossible to see if they fall to the floor).

Cut a length of the floss you intend to use first, at least a yard. Carefully separate out three strands (unless otherwise noted). Place several inches of the floss into the opening of the threader.

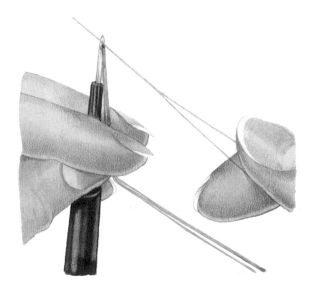

Punching the design

Check the thread to make sure there is nothing
to restrict its flow through the needle as you punch.
A knot or tangle in the thread can be impossible
to remove from the needle casing.

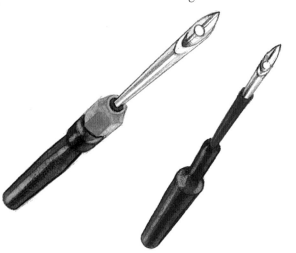

Set your needle for the gauge (depth of loop) you
want. Place the needle where you want to start
punching. Hold the needle almost perpendicular to
the fabric, with the beveled side facing toward
where you will punch. If you are right-handed, you
will punch from right to left; if you are left-handed,
you will punch from left to right.

Firmly push the needle all the way down until it
stops. Bring the needle back up, keeping the tip in
contact with the fabric to avoid pulling your loop
back up. Drag the needle to the next place you
want to punch. Leave an opening or two between

the stitches; you want a continuous but uncrowded
line of loops on the "good" side of the weaver's
cloth. After you have several stitches in, leave your
needle in the pushed-down position and trim off
the "tail" from the first stitch, flush with the fabric.
If you want to check your loops for height and
spacing, keep the needle down while you turn the
the hoop over. When you resume stitching, make
sure the bevel faces the next stitch.

Continue punching in a smooth row, "punch, lift,
drag, punch."

If you are punching an object, such as a leaf or petal, punch a row just inside the line to outline the object. Then fill it by adding rows of punching, following the object's shape and leaving about a needle's width of space between rows. When you change direction, hold the needle stationary and turn the hoop; this keeps the bevel facing the correct direction.

When you finish an area, never drag the thread to the next place you want to punch, even if it is the same color. While the needle is down, turn the hoop over to the front side. Back the needle out just a little (you want it to remain threaded), and use sharp pointed scissors to clip the threads even with the top of your loops so they become part of the pile. Move to the next area you want to punch.

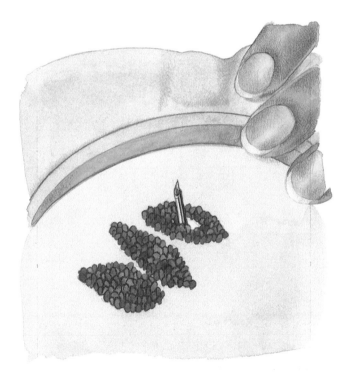

When you need to go to another color, unthread and rethread the needle with the new color. Or, have several needles on hand, each threaded with a different color.

If you make a mistake, pull out the stitches. Use your finger to rub the weave of the cloth back into place, discard the used thread, and punch the stitches again. When you finish, clip any stray ends.

Punch Needle Miniature Album Quilt

Finished size: 30" x 30"

Assembling the Quilt

A symbol of hospitality, pineapples were appliquéd in green and gold on the four corners of the original Horse and Birds Album Quilt *to set a theme of welcoming friendship to guests. It is possible that the generously-sized 98" x 101" quilt was made especially as a guest-room spread. The quilt is replicated here in punch needle blocks and sewn borders that combine to make a quilt that measures a mere 30" x 30". Individual blocks are suitable for framing, or the miniature masterpiece quilt can be displayed as a welcoming wallhanging for your friends and family.*

Materials

25—5-1/2" x 5-1/2" punched block squares from patterns on pages 79–90

15 punched birds (13 yellow and 2 red) from pattern on page 91

1-1/2 yards of white fabric

1/3 yard of red fabric

34" x 34" square of batting

Cut the Fabric

From white, cut:

34" x 34" backing square

4—1-1/4" x 44" middle border strips

4—2" x 44" binding strips

From red, cut:

4—1-1/2" x 44" inner border strips

4—1" x 44" outer border strips

All measurements include 1/4" seam allowances. Sew with right sides together unless otherwise specified.

Assemble the Quilt Center

1. Referring to the photograph, opposite, and to the Block and Bird Placement Diagram on page 28, lay out the 5-1/2" x 5 1/2" punch needle blocks on a flat surface in 5 rows of 5 blocks each.

2. Sew the blocks together in rows. Press the seam allowances of each row to one side, alternating the direction with each row.

3. Sew the rows together to complete the quilt center.

Assemble the Quilt Top

1. Measure the quilt center length as shown in Diagram A, and cut two 1-1/2"-wide red inner border strips to this length. Sew the inner border to the left and right edges of the quilt center. Press the seam allowances toward the borders.

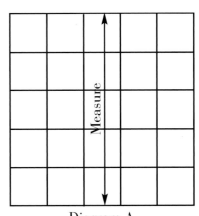

Diagram A

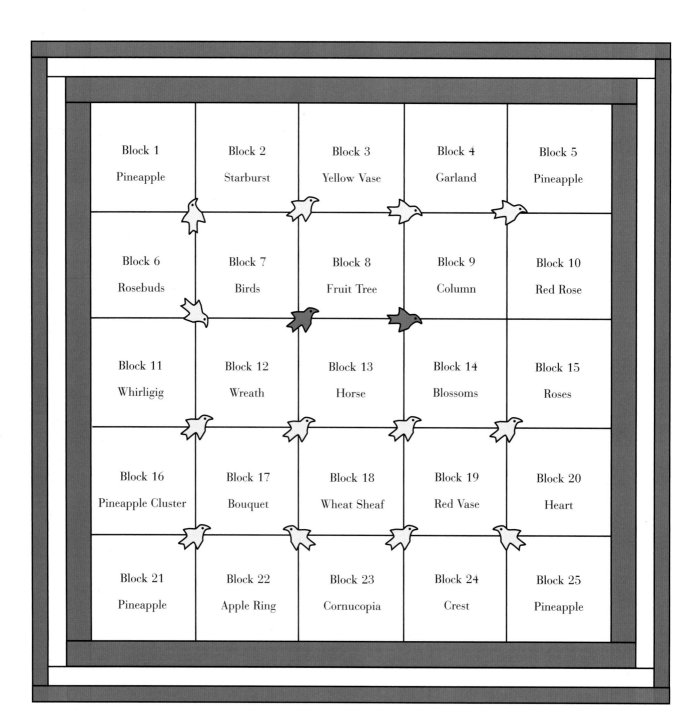

Block and Bird Placement Diagram

2. Measure the quilt width through the center, including the inner borders as shown in Diagram B. Cut two 1-1/2"-wide red inner border strips to this length. Sew the inner borders to the top and bottom edges of the quilt center. Press the seam allowances toward the borders.

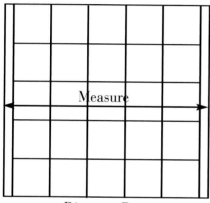

Diagram B

3. Measure the quilt length, including the inner borders. Cut two middle borders from the 1-1/4"-wide white strips. Sew the middle borders to the left and right edges of the quilt. Press the seam allowances away from the center.

4. Measure the quilt width, including the borders. Cut two middle borders to this length from the remaining 1-1/4"-wide white strips. Sew the borders to the top and bottom edges of the quilt. Press the seam allowances away from the center.

5. Measure the quilt length, including the borders. Cut two 1"-wide red outer border strips to this length. Sew the outer borders to the left and right edges of the quilt. Press the seam allowances toward the outer borders.

6. Measure the quilt width, including all borders. Cut two 1"-wide red outer border strips to this length. Sew the outer borders to the top and bottom edges of the quilt. Press the seam allowances toward the outer borders.

Complete the Quilt

1. Smooth out the backing on a flat surface, with the wrong side up, and center the batting on the backing. Center the quilt top, right side up, on the batting. Baste the layers together.

2. Thread your machine with white thread. Beginning in the center and working outward, machine-quilt as close as possible to outline each punch needle shape. Continue adding parallel lines about 3/16" apart to completely fill the white background of the quilt center with echo quilting. For the borders, quilt zigzag lines 3/8" apart to fill all the borders.

3. Trim about 1/4" beyond each bird shape. Turn under the fabric and hand-appliqué the birds to the quilt top near the intersections of the blocks, referring to the Block and Bird Placement Diagram on page 28 for placement.

4. Sew the short ends of the 2"-wide white binding strips together with diagonal seams to form one long binding strip. Trim the seam allowances to 1/4" and press open. Fold the strip in half lengthwise with wrong sides together; press.

5. Beginning at the center of the bottom edge, place the binding strip on the right side of the quilt, aligning the raw edges of the binding with the raw edges of the quilt top. Fold the beginning of the binding strip about 1/2". Sew through all layers 1/4" in from the raw edges, mitering the corners. Trim away the excess binding, leaving 1/2" at the end to overlap the beginning of the

strip. Trim the batting and backing even with the quilt top.

6. Fold the binding to the back of the wall quilt to cover the machine stitching; press. Slip-stitch the folded edge of the binding in place.

Add the Label

The blocks for this miniature quilt were created by several punch needle specialists, as shown on the label, below. If desired, adding a computer-generated fabric label to the back of the quilt provides an interesting quilt history for future generations.

Quilt Assembly Diagram

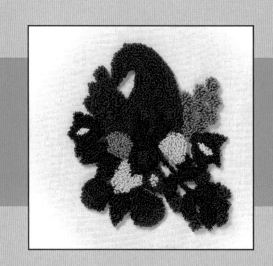

BLOCKS

Pineapple

Punch needle specialist: Sally Van Nuys

Punch Needle
Blocks 1, 5, 21, 25

A symbol of hospitality, pineapples were appliquéd in green and gold on the four corners of the quilt to set a theme of welcoming friendship to guests.

Materials for each block

A square of weaver's cloth, at least 12" x 12"

Three-strand punch needle and a hoop

Embroidery floss (refer to Color Key)

Punching the Pineapple

1. Referring to Getting Started in Basics, page 22, transfer the full-size pattern (including the 5"-square box) to the weaver's cloth. Patterns have been reversed. Use three strands of floss unless otherwise noted.

2. Thread your needle with the dark green floss, and outline the lower pair of leaves and the stem, just inside the lines. Then outline the top leaves, just inside the lines. Where leaves touch each other at the base, leave about two needle-widths of space between your rows.

3. Following the contours of the outline stitching, fill the outermost sections of the lower leaves and fill the stem. Work two rows inside each top leaf.

4. Thread the needle with just two strands of the light green floss, and work one or two short rows between the leaves to create contrast and separation.

5. Thread the needle with three strands of the light green floss, and fill the open area inside each of the top leaves.

6. Thread the needle with two strands of light green and one strand of dark green floss, and fill the open areas of the lower leaves.

COLOR KEY	AMOUNT	ANCHOR #	DMC #
1 dark green	1 skein	683	500 Very Dark Blue Green
2 light green	4 yards	842	3013 Light Khaki Green
3 variegated gold	3 yards	1243	111 Variegated Gold
4 gold	3 yards	1001	976 Medium Golden Brown

7. Remove one segment of the needle gauge, to make a slightly longer loop. Separate a 1-1/2 yard length of variegated gold floss into two groups of three strands.

8. Thread the needle with the variegated gold floss, and stitch on the lines of the scallops. The longer loops and the variegated floss will add texture.

9. Return to the beginning needle depth, and thread the needle with gold floss. Fill in the scallops and spaces at each side, leaving a small open space in the center of each scallop (see the dots on the pattern).

10. Again remove one segment to make a slightly longer loop. Cut a length of variegated gold and thread just one strand of the darkest shade. Stitch three loops at each dot to form the eyes of the pineapple.

11. Carefully trim any loose threads.

Starburst

Punch needle specialist: Charlotte Dudney

Punch Needle Block 2

With a variety of flowers that look fresh-picked from the garden, the Starburst bouquet displays a wonderful balance of color and form. Interestingly, the red "starburst" flower appears to be inspired by a classic quilt block, the Ohio Star.

Materials

A square of weaver's cloth, at least 12" x 12"

Three-strand punch needle and a hoop

Embroidery floss (refer to Color Key)

Punching the Starburst

1. Referring to Getting Started in Basics, page 22, transfer the full-size pattern (including the 5"-square box) to the weaver's cloth. Patterns have been reversed. Use three strands of floss unless otherwise noted.

2. Thread your needle with the dark green floss, and punch the stems. Use a double row of punching, placed close together so it looks like one solid, thick row.

3. Punch the leaves and the bases of the flowers, outlining and then filling by following the contour lines.

4. Thread your needle with the red floss. Outline and fill the flower shapes; wait to punch the red areas within the leaves and flowers.

5. Thread your needle with the gold floss. Outline and fill the three gold flower shapes.

COLOR KEY	AMOUNT	ANCHOR #	DMC #
1 dark green	1 skein	683	500 Very Dark Blue Green
5 red	5-1/2 yards	1098	349 Dark Coral
4 gold	3 yards	1001	976 Medium Golden Brown

6. While you still have gold floss in the needle, fill in the center of the small red flower.

7. Thread the needle with the red floss again, and punch the red centers of the green leaves and gold flowers.

8. Carefully trim any loose threads.

Tip: Gently "rake" the finished project to separate the colors.

Yellow Vase

Punch needle specialist: Karen Gates

Punch Needle Block 3

The perfect symmetry of this sunny bouquet complements the overall design of the Horse and Birds Album Quilt. *In the quilt itself, the white flowers are formed by intricate quilting that shapes the blooms.*

Materials

A square of weaver's cloth, at least 12" x 12"

Three-strand punch needle and a hoop

Embroidery floss (refer to Color Key)

Punching the Yellow Vase

1. Referring to Getting Started in Basics, page 22, transfer the full-size pattern (including the 5"-square box) to the weaver's cloth. Patterns have been reversed. Use three strands of floss unless otherwise noted.

2. Thread your needle with the yellow floss, and punch the vase. Outline and fill in, following the shape of the vase. Shaping the punching in this way will make the vase look rounded on the "good" side of the block. Remember to punch the two small yellow areas that are part of the lip of the vase.

3. Punch the yellow centers of the top flowers.

4. Change to red floss, and punch all the red areas, outlining and filling in. When you fill in the large red flowers, work toward the center, following the shape.

5. Using the pink floss, outline and fill the pink flower parts.

COLOR KEY	AMOUNT	ANCHOR #	DMC #
6 yellow	5 yards	295	3822 Light Straw
5 red	1 skein	1098	349 Dark Coral
7 pink	1/2 yard	25	3354 Light Antique Rose
8 ecru	2 yards	926	712 Ecru
1 dark green	1 skein	683	500 Very Dark Blue Green

6. Using the ecru floss, punch the white flowers. Outline them and fill them by following the contour of the flowers.

7. Thread the needle with dark green floss, and punch all the leaves and the stems of the red flowers. In each case, outline with a single row of stitches and then fill, following the shape of the leaf or stem.

8. Carefully trim any loose threads.

Tip: Gently "rake" the finished project to separate the colors.

Garland

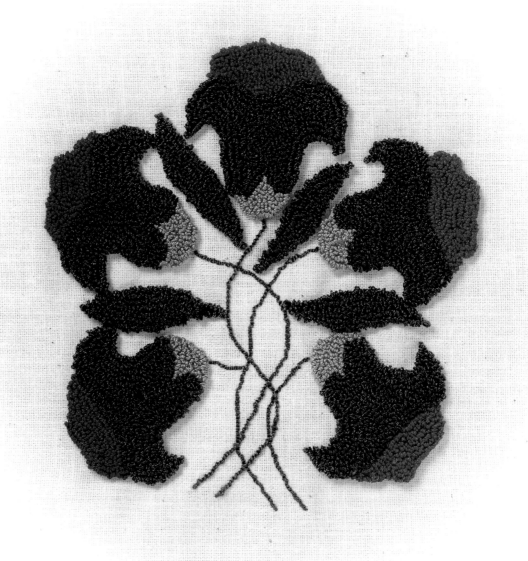

Punch needle specialist: Karen Gates

Punch Needle Block 4

The quilter chose to place only four leaves and four vining stems among the five identical flowers of the garland. Careful asymmetrical placement of leaves and stems creates an interesting contrast with the flowers and establishes an overall balance.

Materials
A square of weaver's cloth, at least 12" x 12"

Three-strand punch needle and a hoop

Embroidery floss (refer to Color Key)

Punching the Garland

1. Referring to Getting Started in Basics, page 22, transfer the full-size pattern (including the 5"-square box) to the weaver's cloth. Patterns have been reversed. Use three strands of floss unless otherwise noted.

2. Thread your needle with the gold floss, and outline and fill the gold portion of each flower. Follow the shape of the area.

3. Change to dark green floss, and punch all the dark green areas next. For each flower or leaf part, outline the object, and fill it by working inward, following the shape of the object.

4. Still using dark green floss, punch the stems, using a single line of punching.

Tip: An effective technique for creating a very thin line is to punch the stems in "reverse punching," which means you turn your hoop to the right side of the pattern and punch down to the wrong side. This makes

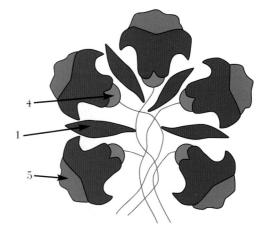

COLOR KEY	AMOUNT	ANCHOR #	DMC #
4 gold	2 yards	1001	976 Medium Golden Brown
1 dark green	1-1/2 skeins	683	500 Very Dark Blue Green
5 red	6 yards	1098	349 Dark Coral

a line of stitches on the right side of the pattern, with the loops on the wrong side. If you choose to do this, you need to draw the lines of the stems very lightly on the right side and stay precisely on the lines when you punch.

5. Now thread the needle with red floss, and punch the flowers, outlining and filling, following the shape.

6. Carefully trim any loose threads.

Tip: Gently "rake" the finished project to separate the colors.

Rosebuds

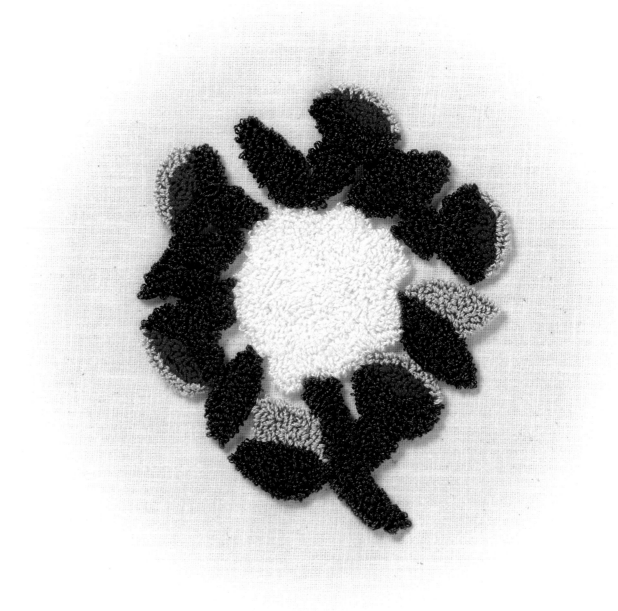

Punch needle specialist: April Mathis

Punch Needle Block 6

The quilt from which these designs are drawn is a masterpiece of quilting, with intricacy and skill that are hard to match. In this cluster of rosebuds, the white center, composed of hundreds of tiny stitches, was made solely by the quilter's needle.

Materials

A square of weaver's cloth, at least 12" x 12"

Three-strand punch needle and a hoop

Embroidery floss (refer to Color Key)

Punching the Rosebuds

1. Referring to Getting Started in Basics, page 22, transfer the full-size pattern (including the 5"-square box) to the weaver's cloth. Patterns have been reversed. Use three strands of floss unless otherwise noted.

2. Thread your needle with the white floss. Outline the large white center, and then work inwards, punching along the contours of the shape. You will need to make about 10 concentric rows.

3. Change to the dark green floss and punch the dark green leaves, buds, and stems. (Note that two leaves are to be pink.) On the stems and the narrow ends of the buds, stay inside the lines to contain the loops more closely. For each leaf, bud, and stem, outline the object and then fill it by following the shape of the object.

COLOR KEY	AMOUNT	ANCHOR #	DMC #
9 white	1 skein	70	3865 Winter White
1 dark green	1 skeins	683	500 Very Dark Blue Green
5 red	2 yards	1098	349 Dark Coral
7 pink	2 yards	25	3354 Light Antique Rose

4. Using red floss, outline and fill the red areas on the buds.

5. Using pink floss, outline the pink leaves and fill them, following their shape. Add the pink tops to the rosebuds, just two rows of punching.

6. Carefully trim any loose threads.

Tip: Gently "rake" the finished project to separate the colors.

Birds

Punch needle specialist: Linda Repasky

Punch Needle Block 7

In a lively variation on the "wreath" theme, red birds encircle a nest holding eggs.
The quilter added a bit of unnatural whimsy—the nest is pink.

Materials

A square of weaver's cloth, at least 12" x 12"

Three-strand punch needle and a hoop

Embroidery floss (refer to Color Key)

Punching the Birds

1. Referring to Getting Started in Basics, page 22, transfer the full-size pattern (including the 5"-square box) to the weaver's cloth. Patterns have been reversed. Use three strands of floss unless otherwise noted.

Note: the amounts of floss allow for making the quilt's two "free-flying" red birds as well as the seven birds that are part of this block.

2. Thread your needle with pink floss, and start with the nest. Punch a single row of loops to outline the nest, and then fill in with rows that follow the contours.

3. Change to tan floss, and punch the three eggs. For each, outline the egg and then add a small circle of punching to fill.

4. Using dark green floss, work the leaves around the nest. Treat each triangular leaf as a unit, punching a single row to outline the leaf and then filling it in.

5. Continuing with the dark green floss, punch two rows of loops along the upper edge of the nest, from one end to the other.

6. Move next to the dark green leaves at the corners. For each pair, punch a single row to outline the pair, and then fill them in, following the contour of the leaves.

COLOR KEY	AMOUNT	ANCHOR #	DMC #
7 pink	2 yards	25	3354 Light Antique Rose
10 tan	6 yards	943	422 Hazelnut Brown
1 dark green	6 yards	683	500 Very Dark Blue Green
11 black	1 yard	403	310 Black
9 white	1 yard	70	3865 Winter White
5 red	2-1/2 skeins	1098	349 Dark Coral

7. Begin with the birds' eyes. Thread your needle with just one strand of black floss, for the pupil of the eye. For each bird, punch three loops very close together in the center of the eye and clip the floss.

8. Thread the needle with three strands of white floss. For each bird, punch a single row of loops in a circle around the pupil.

9. Now thread the needle with red floss for the birds' bodies. For each bird, outline the bird with a single row of loops, and then fill in the bird, echoing the outline of its body shape.

10. Carefully trim any loose threads.

Fruit Tree

Punch needle specialist: Helen Stetina

Punch Needle Block 8

One of the joys of summer and early autumn is picking fresh fruit from the trees in the orchard. And what a bumper crop this tree displays.

Materials

A square of weaver's cloth, at least 12" x 12"

Three-strand punch needle and a hoop

Embroidery floss (refer to Color Key)

Punching the Fruit Tree

1. Referring to Getting Started in Basics, page 22, transfer the full-size pattern (including the 5"-square box) to the weaver's cloth. Patterns have been reversed. Use three strands of floss unless otherwise noted.

Cutting Tip: When you start a motif, cut about 2 yards of floss. As you near completion of that motif and see that not very much more floss is required, you can cut just 1 yard.

2. Thread your needle with the dark green floss, and begin by outlining the tree.

3. Fill in the dark green of the tree, working from the outside in. Follow the shapes of the apples, and use extra lines to complete the filling between apples. (Again, be very careful to punch inside the lines.)

4. Change to red floss, and punch the apples and the red flowers. For the apples, a spiral works well, starting with a complete circle and continuing with another circle and an end to fill the middle of the apple.

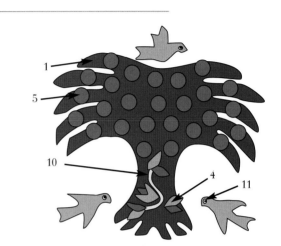

COLOR KEY	AMOUNT	ANCHOR #	DMC #
1 dark green	1-1/2 skeins	683	500 Very Dark Blue Green
5 red	6 yards	1098	349 Dark Coral
10 tan	1 yard	943	422 Hazelnut Brown
4 gold	4 yards	1001	976 Medium Golden Brown
11 black	1/2 yard	403	310 Black

5. Using tan floss, punch a closely-spaced double line of stitching along the vine on the trunk.

6. Using gold floss, outline and fill in the remaining leaves.

7. Outline the birds with gold floss, keeping points as sharp as you can, and then fill in the birds, following their shape. For the birds' eyes, either punch two loops with a dark floss or use a sewing needle and take two stitches with one strand of black floss.

8. Carefully trim any loose threads.

Tip: Gently "rake" the finished project to separate the colors.

Column

Punch needle specialist: Helen Stetina

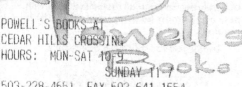

POWELL'S BOOKS AT
CEDAR HILLS CROSSING
HOURS: MON-SAT 10-9
           SUNDAY 11-7
503-228-4651 FAX 503-641-1554

QTY	SKU	PRICE
1	Getting Started In Punch Ne	7.95

Total # of items in this sale: 1

Total Sale $7.95

Cash $10.00

Your Change $2.05

3/10/2015 4:31:25 PM
[Store: 2] [Register: 4] [Cashier: 40]

WE ACCEPT RETURNS WITHIN 30
DAYS OF PURCHASE.
THANK YOU FOR SHOPPING AT
POWELL'S AT CEDAR HILLS
CROSSING!

0011495407

POWELL'S BOOKS
503.228.4651   800.878.7323

powells.com

RETURNS POLICY

POWELL'S BOOKS
503.228.4651   800.878.7323

powells.com

RETURNS POLICY

POWELL'S BOOKS
503.228.4651   800.878.7323

powells.com

RETURNS POLICY

Punch Needle Block 9

During the second quarter of the 1800s, America experienced a revival of interest in classical forms, including a Greek Revival in architecture and furnishings. Greek columns were being used in interior architecture around 1840. The quilter's vase, with its symmetrical spiral design, resembles an Ionic column.

Materials

A square of weaver's cloth, at least 12" x 12"

Three-strand punch needle and a hoop

Embroidery floss (refer to Color Key)

Punching the Column

1. Referring to Getting Started in Basics, page 22, transfer the full-size pattern (including the 5"-square box) to the weaver's cloth. Patterns have been reversed. Use three strands of floss unless otherwise noted.

2. Thread your needle with the ecru floss. Begin by filling the white spaces in the column, following the contours of each area.

3. Change to the red floss, and punch the lines of the column, punching fairly closely to establish solid lines.

4. Punch the red flowers, outlining each flower and continuing a spiral into the center.

5. Punch the dark green leaves, outlining and then filling each leaf, following its diamond-shaped contour.

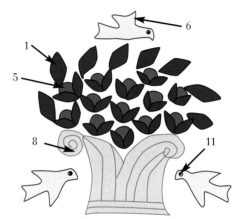

COLOR KEY	AMOUNT	ANCHOR #	DMC #
8 ecru	1 skein	926	712 Ecru
5 red	4-1/2 yards	1098	349 Dark Coral
1 dark green	6 yards	683	500 Very Dark Blue Green
6 yellow	5 yards	295	3822 Light Straw
11 black	1/2 yard	403	310 Black

6. Using the yellow floss, outline and fill the three birds. To add the eyes, punch two loops of black floss, or use a regular sewing needle to make a couple stitches with one strand of black floss.

7. Carefully trim any loose threads.

Tip: Gently "rake" the finished project to separate the colors.

Red Rose

Punch needle specialist: April Mathis

Punch Needle Block 10

The stylized red rose is set off by a circle of buds, botanically unrealistic but artistically dramatic. In terms of the overall design of the circa 1840 Horse and Birds Album Quilt, this block appears to complement the rosebuds in the same row.

Materials

A square of weaver's cloth, at least 12" x 12"

Three-strand punch needle and a hoop

Embroidery floss (refer to Color Key)

Punching the Red Rose

1. Referring to Getting Started in Basics, page 22, transfer the full-size pattern (including the 5"-square box) to the weaver's cloth. Patterns have been reversed. Use three strands of floss unless otherwise noted.

2. Thread your needle with the red floss. Begin with the large flower; outline it, and then fill it in, working toward the center in concentric rings that echo the shape of the flower. It will take about 12 rows to fill the flower, plus a few stitches in the center.

3. While you have red floss in the needle, go on to outline and fill the rosebuds, and then punch a tiny double row in the red area of the leaf.

COLOR KEY	AMOUNT	ANCHOR #	DMC #
5 red	6 yards	1098	349 Dark Coral
1 dark green	1 skein	683	500 Very Dark Blue Green

4. Change to the green floss and punch all the green areas of leaves and stems. For each, outline the object and then fill it, following the contours of the object.

5. Carefully trim any loose threads.

Tip: Gently "rake" the finished project to separate the colors.

Whirligig

Punch needle specialist: April Mathis

Punch Needle Block 11

The whirligig has been a perennial favorite for children as a toy and for quilters as an appliqué motif. As a block pattern, it offers interest and a sense of movement, and it ties the design elements together through the bold use of red and green.

Materials

A square of weaver's cloth, at least 12" x 12"

Three-strand punch needle and a hoop

Embroidery floss (refer to Color Key)

Punching the Whirligig

1. Referring to Getting Started in Basics, page 22, transfer the full-size pattern (including the 5"-square box) to the weaver's cloth. Patterns have been reversed. Use three strands of floss unless otherwise noted.

2. Start with the whirligig's center medallion, working from the outside to the red center. Thread your needle with the gold floss, and punch the gold portion. When you finish, "rake" the floss together on the front side of the weaver's cloth to make a distinct edge.

3. Change to the dark green floss, and punch just one row inside the gold. Again, rake the dark green to get a distinct line.

4. Change to the red floss, and fill the center of the medallion.

5. Outline and fill the red leaves. When you fill them, follow the shape of each lobe of the leaf. You will have a narrow area of

COLOR KEY	AMOUNT	ANCHOR #	DMC #
4 gold	1/2 yard	1001	976 Medium Golden Brown
1 dark green	1 skein	683	500 Very Dark Blue Green
5 red	1 skein	1098	349 Dark Coral

unpunched fabric remaining in the center of each leaf.

6. Change back to the green floss, and outline and fill the green leaves. After the leaves are finished, fold the leaves lengthwise so the unpunched fabric area is opened up, and push the loops back against the leaf to make a more distinct white area.

7. Carefully trim any loose threads.

Tip: Gently "rake" the finished project to separate the colors.

Wreath

Punch needle specialist: Marilyn Lopez

Punch Needle
Block 12

In the original quilt, the four red flowers and the leaves of the wreath are appliquéd, as are the centers for the white flowers. The white flowers themselves, however, are not made of appliquéd fabric. They are formed by the intricate quilting detail that characterizes this antique quilt.

Materials

A square of weaver's cloth, at least 12" x 12"

Three-strand punch needle and a hoop

Embroidery floss (refer to Color Key)

Punching the Wreath

1. Referring to Getting Started in Basics, page 22, transfer the full-size pattern (including the 5"-square box) to the weaver's cloth. Patterns have been reversed. Use three strands of floss unless otherwise noted.

2. Thread your needle with the red floss, and outline and fill the middle of each white flower, following the shape.

3. Change to the dark green floss, and outline and fill the middle of each red flower, following the shape.

4. Outline and fill in the leaves, following the shapes.

5. Punch the stems of the flowers.

Tip: If you have a one-strand punch needle, use it to punch the stems for finer detail.

6. Return to the red floss, and punch the red flowers, outlining and filling, following the

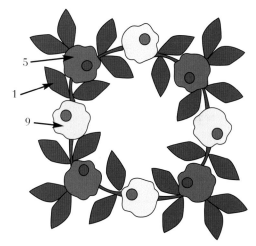

COLOR KEY	AMOUNT	ANCHOR #	DMC #
5 red	4-1/2 yards	1098	349 Dark Coral
1 dark green	2 skeins	683	500 Very Dark Blue Green
9 white	4-1/2 yards	70	3865 Winter White

shape. You can use a very long spiral for each flower, working toward the center in concentric circles.

7. Using the white floss, punch the white flowers, outlining and filling them in the same way you did the red.

8. Carefully trim any loose threads.

Tip: Gently "rake" the finished project to separate the colors.

Horse

Punch needle specialist: Marilyn Lopez

Punch Needle Block 13

Horses, and their pastures, have long been central to the Maryland culture and economy. To this day, sections of Maryland are "horse country." In some early portraits of horses, the pose is exactly that of our Maryland quilter's horse: One foreleg raised, head up, and tail flying.

Materials

A square of weaver's cloth, at least 12" x 12"

Three-strand punch needle and a hoop

Embroidery floss (refer to Color Key)

Punching the Horse

1. Referring to Getting Started in Basics, page 22, transfer the full-size pattern (including the 5"-square box) to the weaver's cloth. Patterns have been reversed. Use three strands of floss unless otherwise noted.

2. Thread your needle with the red floss, and begin with the horse. Outline the entire horse, and then follow the contours as you fill in the horse. Leave a small area open for the eye, which you will add later.

3. Outline and fill the three small red circles above the horse, and punch the red leaves in the grass below the horse.

4. Change to the gold floss, and punch the gold leaves in the grass.

5. Outline and fill in the gold circles over the horse. Follow the circle shape for each.

6. Using the dark green floss, outline and fill all the dark green shapes. In each shape, follows its contour as you fill.

COLOR KEY	AMOUNT	ANCHOR #	DMC #
5 red	7 yards	1098	349 Dark Coral
4 gold	5 yards	1001	976 Medium Golden Brown
1 dark green	1 skein	683	500 Very Dark Blue Green
7 pink	1 yard	25	3354 Light Antique Rose
6 yellow	1 yard	295	3822 Light Straw
11 black	scrap	403	310 Black

7. Using red floss, add the red portion of the flower on each side.

8. Punch the pink area on the side flowers by outlining the long outer edge and filling the center with two shorter lines of punching.

9. Using black floss, punch just two stitches for the horse's eye.

10. Carefully trim any loose threads.

Tip: Gently "rake" the finished project to separate the colors.

Blossoms

Punch needle specialist: Marilyn Lopez

Punch Needle Block 14

Cheerful yellow centers brighten the red blossoms on this wreath. An interesting feature of the composition of the circa 1840 Horse and Birds Album Quilt *is that with thoughtful consideration, none of the numerous floral wreath blocks are placed adjacent to one another.*

Materials

A square of weaver's cloth, at least 12" x 12"

Three-strand punch needle and a hoop

Embroidery floss (refer to Color Key)

Punching the Blossoms

1. Referring to Getting Started in Basics, page 22, transfer the full-size pattern (including the 5"-square box) to the weaver's cloth. Patterns have been reversed. Use three strands of floss unless otherwise noted.

2. Thread your needle with the yellow floss, and outline and fill the center of each flower, following the shape of the center.

3. Change to the red floss, and outline and fill each flower, following the shape.

4. Using the dark green floss, outline and fill the leaves, following the diamond shape of the leaf.

5. Carefully trim any loose threads.

Tip: Gently "rake" the finished project to separate the colors.

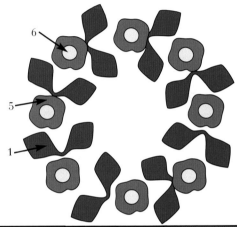

COLOR KEY	AMOUNT	ANCHOR #	DMC #
6 yellow	1-1/2 yards	295	3822 Light Straw
5 red	6 yards	1098	349 Dark Coral
1 dark green	1-1/2 skeins	683	500 Very Dark Blue Green

Roses

Punch needle specialist: April Mathis

Punch Needle Block 15

Using a slightly stronger red than is used on most of the floral motifs in the blocks of the circa 1840 Horse and Birds Album Quilt provides greater contrast between the pink and the red roses. The dashes of color in the leaves add spice.

Materials

A square of weaver's cloth, at least 12" x 12"

Three-strand punch needle and a hoop

Embroidery floss (refer to Color Key)

Punching the Roses

1. Referring to Getting Started in Basics, page 22, transfer the full-size pattern (including the 5"-square box) to the weaver's cloth. Patterns have been reversed. Use three strands of floss unless otherwise noted.

2. Thread your needle with the pink floss to punch the two pink flowers. Outline and fill each flower, working toward the center and following the contour of the flower.

3. Still using pink, punch the dash of pink in two of the leaves. You need only to outline the patch and add one short row in the middle.

4. Change to the red floss, and punch the two red flowers. Outline and fill each flower, working toward the center and following the contour of the flower.

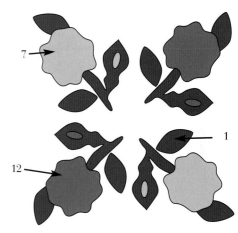

COLOR KEY	AMOUNT	ANCHOR #	DMC #
7 pink	1 skein	25	3354 Light Antique Rose
12 dark red	1 skein	1025	347 Very Dark Salmon
1 dark green	1 skein	683	500 Very Dark Blue Green

5. Punch the dash of red in the leaves as you did the pink patches.

6. Change to the dark green floss, and work the stems and leaves. Stay inside the lines of the stems so they do not get too wide. For each stem and leaf, outline and fill it, following the shape of the object.

7. Carefully trim any loose threads.

Tip: Gently "rake" the finished project to separate the colors.

Pineapple Cluster

Punch needle specialist: Kristan DiBiase

Punch Needle Block 16

The pineapples at the four corners of the quilt set the theme of hospitality, and the graceful pineapple cluster repeats the theme. In nature, pineapples do not grow on stems, but in quilting—as in most art—the quilter's reality rules.

Materials

A square of weaver's cloth, at least 12" x 12"

Three-strand punch needle and a hoop

Embroidery floss (refer to Color Key)

Punching the Pineapple Cluster

1. Referring to Getting Started in Basics, page 22, transfer the full-size pattern (including the 5"-square box) to the weaver's cloth. Patterns have been reversed. Use three strands of floss unless otherwise noted.

2. Thread your needle with the dark green floss, and begin with the dark leaves. Outline each leaf and work in toward the center, following the shape of the leaf.

3. Change to the gold floss, and outline and fill the pineapples. Again, work in toward the center, following the contour of the pineapple.

4. Using the avocado green, outline and fill the remaining pineapple leaves and the leaves along the stems.

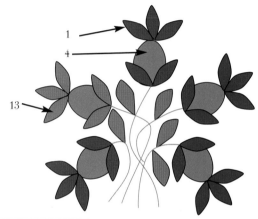

COLOR KEY	AMOUNT	ANCHOR #	DMC #
1 dark green	1 skein	683	500 Very Dark Blue Green
4 gold	1 skein	1001	976 Medium Golden Brown
13 avocado green	1 skein	267	469 Avocado Green

5. Punch the stems, one row, right on the line. Saving the stems for last helps the floss stay in line.

6. Carefully trim any loose threads.

Tip: Gently "rake" the finished project to separate the colors.

Bouquet

Punch needle specialist: Charlotte Dudney

Punch Needle Block 17

In the circa 1840 Horse and Birds Album Quilt, the stylized vase is similar to pottery that appears as an appliqué motif in other early Album quilts.

Materials

A square of weaver's cloth, at least 12" x 12"

Three-strand punch needle and a hoop

Embroidery floss (refer to Color Key)

Punching the Bouquet

1. Referring to Getting Started in Basics, page 22, transfer the full-size pattern (including the 5"-square box) to the weaver's cloth. Patterns have been reversed. Use three strands of floss unless otherwise noted.

2. Thread your needle with the dark green floss, and outline and then fill the leaves and stems, following the contours. Spacing between the rows is very important. Leaving a needle-width of space between rows ensures that they lie flat.

3. Thread your needle with the red floss, and punch the red flowers, outlining them and then following their contour to fill them.

4. Outline the red vase, and then fill it in. There are several contour lines to follow as you fill: The wavy lines at the top and bottom, the sloped lines of the sides, and the shapes of the "slots" at the bottom of the base.

5. Outline and fill the red birds, again following the contours. Leave a small space for the eyes.

6. Thread your needle with the pink floss. Outline and fill the central pink flower.

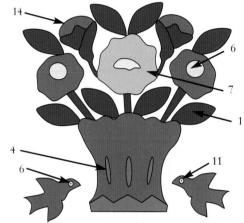

COLOR KEY	AMOUNT	ANCHOR #	DMC #
14 dark coral	1-1/4 skein	1098	349 Dark Coral
4 gold	2 yards	1001	976 Medium Golden Brown
6 yellow	1 yard	295	3822 Light Straw
7 pink	3 yards	25	3354 Light Antique Rose
1 dark green	7 yards	683	500 Very Dark Blue Green
11 black	scrap	403	310 Black
9 white	scrap	70	3865 Winter White

7. Thread your needle with the yellow floss. Punch the centers of the three large flowers.

8. Thread your needle with the gold floss. Fill in the slots of the vase, just one line of punching around the edge and one line down the middle, and then complete the bottom of the base, outlining and then filling along the contours.

9. For the birds' eyes, thread an ordinary sewing needle with white floss and make two or three small loops. Then thread the needle with black floss, and make just one loop in the center.

10. Carefully trim any loose threads.

Wheat Sheaf

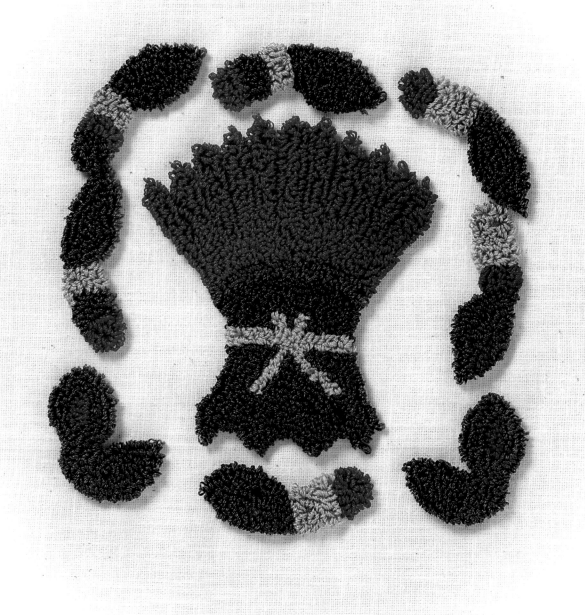

Punch needle specialist: Laura DiBiase

Punch Needle Block 18

At harvest time the plump sheaf of wheat and the fruits of the garden were the fulfillment of the year's hard work in the yet unmechanized farm of the 1840s.

Materials

A square of weaver's cloth, at least 12" x 12"

Three-strand punch needle and a hoop

Embroidery floss (refer to Color Key)

Punching the Wheat Sheaf

1. Referring to Getting Started in Basics, page 22, transfer the full-size pattern (including the 5"-square box) to the weaver's cloth. Patterns have been reversed. Use three strands of floss unless otherwise noted.

2. Thread your needle with dark green floss, and punch the two sections of the very dark green portion of the sheaf, outlining and then filling, following the shape in each section.

3. Change to the dark avocado green floss, and punch the band above the dark green. Outline the band and punch just one more row to fill the band.

4. Using red floss, punch the wheat stalks. Outline the entire red area, starting along the top of the dark avocado green band and continuing around each stalk.

5. Fill the red area. Punch down a stalk toward the green band, work up toward the next stalk by using wavy lines to fill the area under the two stalks, and then punch a row up the center of the second stalk, stopping and starting several times. When you punch the center of a stalk,

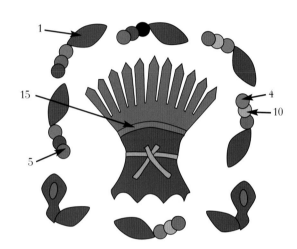

COLOR KEY		AMOUNT	ANCHOR #	DMC #
1	dark green	1-1/2 skeins	683	500 Very Dark Blue Green
15	dark avocado green	1/2 yard	846	936 Dark Avocado Green
5	red	6-1/2 yards	1098	349 Dark Coral
10	tan	1-1/2 yards	943	422 Hazelnut Brown
4	gold	1-1/2 yards	1001	976 Medium Golden Brown

make a double row of punching toward the top of each stalk.

6. Thread your needle with tan floss and outline all the edges of the rope around the sheaf. Punch an inner row along the main part of the rope (not the ties).

7. For the ring around the sheaf, begin with the dark green leaves, outlining and filling each leaf.

8. Use gold, tan, red, and dark green floss to punch the dots. Punching from the leaf outward makes it easier to keep the colors distinct. Add the red centers of the lower leaves.

9. Carefully trim any loose threads.

Red Vase

Punch needle specialist: Sue McAdoo

Punch Needle
Block 19

The Maryland Album quilts from around 1840 share some classic features such as a vase that holds a formal bouquet. The quilter's design skill is evident in the balance among her three flower-filled vases.

Materials
A square of weaver's cloth, at least 12" x 12"
Three-strand punch needle and a hoop
Embroidery floss (refer to Color Key)

Punching the Red Vase

1. Referring to Getting Started in Basics, page 22, transfer the full-size pattern (including the 5"-square box) to the weaver's cloth. Patterns have been reversed. Use three strands of floss unless otherwise noted.

2. Thread the needle with the red floss. Outline the vase, and continue along the contour lines, working toward the center, to fill the shape.

3. Thread the needle with the dark avocado green floss, and outline and fill the greenery above the vase.

4. Again thread the needle with the red floss. Punch the red flowers that protrude from the greenery, and then punch the large red flower. Work on the large flower from the outside in, following the contours of the flower, and keeping outside the line of the little circle in the middle.

5. Thread the needle with the yellow floss, and add the center of the large red flower.

6. To work the birds, outline and fill them along the contour lines. To add an eye to

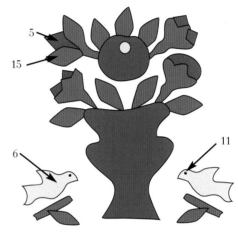

COLOR KEY	AMOUNT	ANCHOR #	DMC #
5 red	1-1/2 skeins	1098	349 Dark Coral
15 dark avocado green	1 skein	846	936 Dark Avocado Green
6 yellow	1 yard	295	3822 Light Straw
11 black	scrap	403	310 Black

each bird, thread a sewing needle with two strands of black floss. Secure the thread beneath the yellow punching. Turn the hoop over and, working from the front side of the weaver's cloth, bring the needle up to make one black loop, return the needle to the underside, and secure the black thread under the yellow.

7. Thread the needle with dark avocado green again, and punch the stems and leaves under the birds.

8. Carefully trim any loose threads.

Tip: Gently "rake" the finished project to separate the colors.

Heart

Punch needle specialist: Helen Stetina

Punch Needle Block 20

Hearts and flowers! For the circa 1840 Horse and Birds Album Quilt, *the quilter cleverly created the heart-shaped wreath by using two birds at the upper corners. The surprisingly contemporary stylized heart adds variety to the overall quilt design while retaining the buds and leaves that contribute to its unity.*

Materials

A square of weaver's cloth, at least 12" x 12"

Three-strand punch needle and a hoop

Embroidery floss (refer to Color Key)

Punching the Heart

1. Referring to Getting Started in Basics, page 22, transfer the full-size pattern (including the 5"-square box) to the weaver's cloth. Patterns have been reversed. Use three strands of floss unless otherwise noted.

2. Thread your needle with the ecru floss, and begin with the interior background. Outline the edges, staying just inside the lines. Fill in the space, following the shape of the background as you work toward the center. Stay outside the lines for the red circles.

3. Change to the dark green floss and punch the top elements of the heart wreath. Because the birds and the heart-shaped connector tend to flow into one another, outline each object inside the lines and follow the contours of each as you fill them.

4. Using the dark green, punch the rest of the heart wreath. Outline it all as one unit, along both inner and outer edges, and then fill, again following the contours.

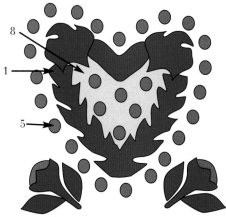

COLOR KEY	AMOUNT	ANCHOR #	DMC #
8 ecru	4 yards	926	712 Ecru
1 dark green	1-1/2 yards	683	500 Very Dark Blue Green
5 red	5 yards	1098	349 Dark Coral

5. While your needle is threaded with dark green, outline and fill the stems, leaves, and buds under the heart.

6. Change to red floss, and punch the circles within the heart wreath and the circles around it, using a spiral to outline and fill each circle.

7. Outline the red buds and fill them with just one line.

8. With a bit of black or gray floss or sewing thread, add two loops to make an eye for each bird.

9. Carefully trim any loose threads.

Tip: Gently "rake" the finished project to separate the colors.

Apple Ring

Punch needle specialist: Marilyn Lopez

Punch Needle Block 22

An element that unifies the design of the circa 1840 Horse and Birds Album Quilt is the use of the stylized wreath. In the Apple Ring, the eight apples are joined by stems and pairs of leaves, arranged in gentle V-shapes— a design feature that unifies the ring itself.

Materials

A square of weaver's cloth, at least 12" x 12"

Three-strand punch needle and a hoop

Embroidery floss (refer to Color Key)

Punching the Apple Ring

1. Referring to Getting Started in Basics, page 22, transfer the full-size pattern (including the 5"-square box) to the weaver's cloth. Patterns have been reversed. Use three strands of floss unless otherwise noted.

2. Thread your needle with the red floss. For each apple, outline the apple and fill it with a long spiral of concentric circles that follow the shape of the apple.

3. Change to the dark green floss, and punch a solid line of dark green between the apples.

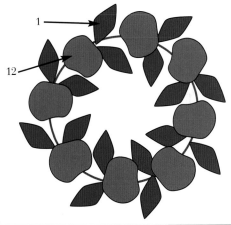

COLOR KEY	AMOUNT	ANCHOR #	DMC #
1 dark green	1 skein	683	500 Very Dark Blue Green
12 dark red	1 skein	1025	347 Very Dark Salmon

4. Punch the leaves, outlining and filling each leaf, following the contour of the leaf.

5. Carefully trim any loose threads.

Tip: Gently "rake" the finished project to separate the colors.

Cornucopia

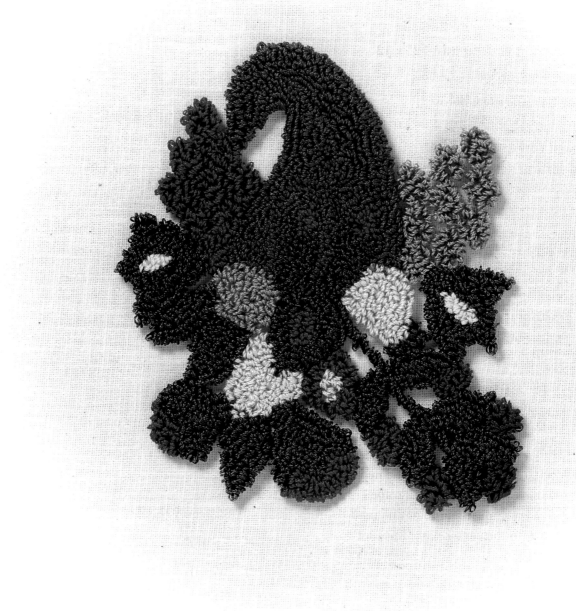

Punch needle specialist: Laura DiBiase

Punch Needle Block 23

The "horn of plenty" harks back to Greek mythology. A "cornu copiae" was a goat's horn overflowing with fruit and flowers. Over the centuries the cornucopia became synonymous with a plentiful harvest, especially at Thanksgiving.

Materials

A square of weaver's cloth, at least 12" x 12"

Three-strand punch needle and a hoop

Embroidery floss (refer to Color Key)

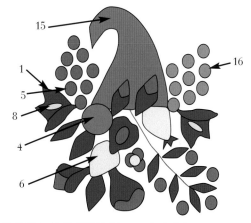

Punching the Cornucopia

1. Referring to Getting Started in Basics, page 22, transfer the full-size pattern (including the 5"-square box) to the weaver's cloth. Patterns have been reversed. Use three strands of floss unless otherwise noted.

2. Thread your needle with the dark avocado green floss, and outline and fill the basket, following its shape and making a sharp point at its end.

3. Change to dark green floss. Punch all the green stems and leaves, carefully remaining inside the lines to avoid overcrowding, especially where the leaves touch the fruit.

4. Use red floss to punch all the red elements. You can use a spiral for each red grape and each cherry, punching the outline and just looping into the center with a partial circle.

5. Using ecru floss, punch a double line inside each of the two leaves that have light centers.

6. Punch the orange, using the tan floss. Outline it with a true circle, and then use a spiral to fill it, working toward the center.

COLOR KEY	AMOUNT	ANCHOR #	DMC #
15 dark avocado green	6 yards	846	936 Dark Avocado Green
1 dark green	1 skein	683	500 Very Dark Blue Green
5 red	4 yards	1098	349 Dark Coral
8 ecru	1/2 yard	926	712 Ecru
4 gold	1 yard	1001	976 Medium Golden Brown
6 yellow	scrap	295	3822 Light Straw
16 steel gray	scrap	235	414 Steel Gray

7. Use the yellow floss to punch the pineapple and the pear and to add a center to the red flower.

8. Punch the second bunch of grapes with the steel gray floss.

9. Carefully trim any loose threads.

Tip: Gently "rake" the finished project to separate the colors.

Crest

Punch needle specialist: Sue McAdoo

Punch Needle Block 24

A bright array of flowers, leaves and delicate stems carries out both the dominant red-and-green color scheme and the balance of circular shapes within the design of the circa 1840 Horse and Birds Album Quilt.

Materials

A square of weaver's cloth, at least 12" x 12"

Three-strand punch needle and a hoop

Embroidery floss (refer to Color Key)

Punching the Crest

1. Referring to Getting Started in Basics, page 22, transfer the full-size pattern (including the 5"-square box) to the weaver's cloth. Patterns have been reversed. Use three strands of floss unless otherwise noted.

2. Thread the needle with dark green floss and punch the stems, punching one row directly on the line and a second row very close to the first, to give enough body to the single-line stems.

3. Punch each dark green leaf, staying within the lines and following the shape of the leaf. Outline the leaf and fill it in, working toward the center.

4. Thread the needle with the red floss, and outline and fill the red leaves.

5. Next punch the red flowers, outlining each petal within the lines and adding a second row to fill the inside of the petal.

COLOR KEY	AMOUNT	ANCHOR #	DMC #
1 dark green	1-1/4 skeins	683	500 Very Dark Blue Green
5 red	1-1/4 skeins	1098	349 Dark Coral
6 yellow	1 yard	295	3822 Light Straw
10 tan	3/4 yard	943	422 Hazelnut Brown

6. Thread the needle with the yellow floss, and punch the centers of the flowers with a circle and one or two central loops.

7. Thread the needle with the tan floss, and punch the small circle at the base of the garland.

8. Carefully trim any loose threads.

Tip: Gently "rake" the finished project to separate the colors.

PATTERNS

Blocks 1,5,21,25

Pineapple

Block 2

Starburst

Block 3
Yellow Vase
19

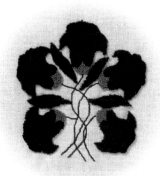

Block 4
Garland
20

Block 6
Rosebuds

Block 7
Birds

Block 8
Fruit Tree

15

Block 9
Column

16

Block 10
Red Rose

Block 11
Whirligig

Block 14
Blossoms

Block 15
Roses

7

Block 16   ✗

Pineapple Cluster

8

Block 17

Bouquet

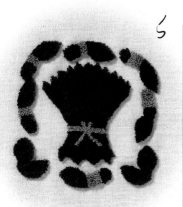

Block 18
Wheat Sheaf

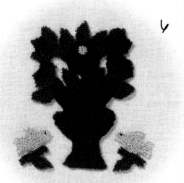

Block 19
Red Vase

Block 20
Heart

4

Block 22
Apple Ring

Block 23
Cornucopia

Block 24
Crest

Birds for Appliqué

Bird Patterns
for Appliqué

The circa 1840 *Horse and Birds Album Quilt*
featured 15 small appliqué bird motifs added to
the quilt after the 25 blocks were assembled. Since
the bird appliqués were positioned facing left and
right in the corners of the blocks, two patterns are
offered here. When transferring the patterns, check
closely to make sure that the motifs are properly
reversed before you begin punching.

You will need to punch 13 yellow birds and 2 red birds.

After the bird motifs have been punched, read
through the instructions for Assembling the Quilt on
page 26 before you cut out the appliqués. Then,
referring to the block and Bird Placement Diagram
on page 28, follow the steps for Completing the
Quilt on page 29.

THE CONTRIBUTORS

Gail Bird

Gail Bird is an innovator, author, lecturer, designer, and teacher who has specialized in the art of Igolochkoy™ (Russian miniature punch needle embroidery) for 30 years. She manufactures and sells authentic tools, and carries a large inventory of books, transfers, patterns, kits, and supplies through Birdhouse Enterprises (www.gailbird.com). She has taught and promoted punch needle in many places around the world, and has recently developed correspondence courses available through her web site.

Her work has been published in many magazines and mentioned in related books. Her own book, *Russian Punchneedle Embroidery*, includes transfers from several designers, 1970s patterns that are especially suitable for use on clothing and linens. Her collection of finished punchneedle work is, she believes, the world's largest.

Birdhouse Enterprises is located in Sacramento, California. It is definitely a family business: Gail and her husband Richard work closely together, and their two daughters and son also have been involved.

Kristan DiBiase

In February 2003, Kristan took a miniature Russian punchneedle class through The Needle Nook in Ligonier PA, with Charlotte Dudney as teacher. Kristan comments, "Charlotte introduced the class by telling the lovely history of the Russian Old Believers, and I eagerly dove into learning how to punch."

During the weekend, as the group of learners punched together and shared several meals, Charlotte mentioned some ways to improve the needle they were using. One improvement, Kristan recalls, was to paint a bit of fingernail polish on the handle so you would always know which direction your needle was facing. The class agreed that would be helpful, and Kristan went home filled with that and other ideas for making a new needle.

With help from her husband, who works in metal designing and manufacturing, she used the suggestions to develop the CTR needle. Their web site is www.ctrneedleworks.com.

Laura DiBiase

Laura DiBiase is a bankruptcy attorney with a passion for needlework. That passion began during law school in 1988 when she first entered The Needle Nook in Ligonier, Pennsylvania. Laura credits Donna McDowell, owner of The Needle Nook in Ligonier, Pennsylvania, with teaching her the numerous varieties of this art form.

In early 2004, Laura flew 3,000 miles to attend a punchneedle class being sponsored by her favorite store, and the obsession took hold. She stitches models for a number of punchneedle designers but, she says, "I try to keep as many for myself as possible!"

Charlotte Dudney

Charlotte Dudney graduated from California Polytechnic State University in 1979 with a Teaching Credential. She has taught primary levels in both public and private schools in several states. She lives in Arlington, Texas, with her husband and daughter.

An accomplished quilt-maker and quilting teacher, Charlotte began learning about punch needle in 2000, while attending a rug-hooking seminar taught by folk artist Leslie McCabe. A year later Charlotte began designing and producing original work for punch needle under the business name "Designs from the Pep'r Pot." Over the last three years, she has taught and promoted Russian punch needle in quilt and needlework shops all over the United States and at major needlework conventions. Her work has been featured in Family Circle Homecraft Magazine and McCall's Quilting magazine.

Charlotte has an extensive line of punchneedle patterns and an instructional video on DVD specifically for punchneedle. Her web site is www.russianpunchneedle.com.

Karen Gates

Folk artist Karen Amadio Gates has been creating needlework of one kind or another since childhood. She first discovered punchneedle embroidery at a folk festival in 2000 and was captivated by its resemblance to miniature hooked rugs. Her original designs are inspired by the work of colonial artisans and are especially suited for use in a doll house.

Karen is a juried member of the Pennsylvania Guild of Craftsmen and was recently selected as one of Early Americana's Best Craftsmen by Historical Publications, Ltd. She also was chosen for inclusion in Early American Life's 2004 Directory of Traditional American Crafts. Her work has been displayed in many gift shops and museums, and she is known as a

speaker, teacher, and demonstrator of the punchneedle craft. Her web site is www.karengatesfolkart.com.

She and her husband Tom live in Bucks County in eastern Pennsylvania, where they are raising sons Tyler and Jordan.

Marilyn Lopez

Marilyn Lopez took her first Russian punchneedle embroidery class two years ago, thinking she would be learning crewel embroidery. She says that, to her surprise, "It was nothing like crewel embroidery. I was willing to learn, and I haven't been able to put my needle down." She has punched several samples for Karen Gates Folk Art Designs. Besides punching, she quilts, crochets, knits, and makes cloth dolls.

Marilyn says that her husband got her started doing needlework. He is originally from Indiana, and they moved there after their marriage eight years ago. Having no family or friends nearby, and with her husband on shift work, she found that she was alone most of the time. Not knowing what to do with herself, since she no longer worked full-time outside the home, she started watching "Simply Quilts." She remembers wishing she could make beautiful quilts "like the ones that danced with colors inside my TV screen." She mentioned her quilting desire to her husband, and a week later he signed her up for a quilting class. "The rest," she says, "is history."

Marilyn lives in Feasterville PA, just outside Philadelphia. She and husband Christian have two children, Katelyn Marie, who is 5, and Christian Michael, who is 3.

April Mathis

April Mathis developed her affection for embroidery when she was 12 years old. She first picked up a set of punch needles at a quilt show in 2001, and has been enthralled with the tool ever since. April teaches punch needle, and she also designs for her own company, Heritage Thread Designs (www.heritagethread.com).

April lives with her husband and two sons in Portland, Maine.

Sue McAdoo

Sue McAdoo says of herself, "I was destined to do needlework!" The love of needlework was passed down from both her mother and father and their families. Quilting, embroidery, crewel, knitting, weaving, rug-braiding, crochet, and machine sewing, just to name a few, were constantly present as she was growing up.

In her early twenties, Sue began to really focus on needlework. Ever since, it has been a passion. She enjoys all types of needlework, including hardanger, pulled thread, open work, canvas work, counted thread, needle tatting, needlepoint and now punchneedle. She took a punchneedle class from Charlotte Dudney—"a super teacher"; Charlotte's enthusiasm rubbed off, and Sue added punch needle to her repertoire.

Sue teaches punchneedle classes at two shops in Pittsburgh, Pennsylvania—the Noble Craftsman in Green Tree and Teatime Stitchery in Monroeville—and also teaches other needle arts, finding each class "a great opportunity to share a little bit of a wonderful craft."

Sue is curriculum coordinator at the Western Pennsylvania School for the Deaf, teaching deaf students and encouraging them to reach their goals. She speaks very appreciatively of her husband John's understanding that needlework is a gift, encouraging her in her needlework endeavors.

Linda Repasky

Linda Repasky is both a rug-hooker and an enthusiast for miniature punchneedle work. She takes business trips; when she found that she was unable to take along her bulky hooking paraphernalia, she pursued miniature punchneedle work. Punch needle quickly developed into a passion as she punched tiny versions of hooked rugs.

Linda now teaches miniature punchneedle classes and workshops nationally and designs punchneedle patterns. She also makes gripper frames that solve the problem of holding punchneedle work exceptionally taut as it is being punched. A sampling of her designs, along with information about the gripper frame, can be seen at www.woolenwhimsies.com.

Linda was selected as one of the country's 200 top artisans for inclusion in Early American Life's 2005 Directory of Traditional American Crafts. She has also written a book on miniature punch needle. She resides in western Massachusetts.

Helen Stetina

Helen Stetina is a full-time sales associate and teacher at The Needle Nook in Ligonier, Pennsylvania, a shop that is a complete source for needlepoint, counted cross-stitch, and most recently, punchneedle embroidery.

Helen added punch needle to her repertoire in 2004 when Charlotte Dudney came to teach a workshop. Shop owner Donna McDowell needed someone to teach classes in punchneedle, and Helen has filled that role. To date, she has taught more than 160 students. Helen also writes the instructions for Barb Carroll's Woolley Fox punchneedle patterns and has punched models for Lee Faulkner of Meme's Cottage Collection. She loves to experiment with using a variety of working frames and finishing techniques, trying different threads, and punching on 18-mesh canvas.

Sally Van Nuys

Ohio artist Sally Van Nuys began collecting antiques as a teenager, and soon found a fondness for primitive antiques, painted decoration, and primitive hooked rugs. In the early 1980s she began painting in the style of folk artists of the past; she also taught decorative painting, stenciling, and theorem painting in her Amherst, Ohio, art studio and shop. Sally opened her online shop in 1998.

In 2002, Sally began rug hooking in the primitive style, using wool strips; Russian punchneedle work followed soon after. Now, when the rug hook is not in her hand, Sally enjoys the quiet slip of the punch needle, creating miniature hooked rugs and other small, original punch needle designs.

Her work has appeared in The Wool Street Journal and Country Marketplace magazines. She regularly contributes original rug hooking and punchneedle projects for Create & Decorate magazine. Sally's work was also selected for Early American Life's 2005 Directory of Traditional American Crafts.

Sally's online shop is Amherst Antiques•Folk Art•Rug Hooking (www.amherst-antiques-folkart.com). She offers classes in both primitive rug hooking and the art of Russian punch needle.

GLOSSARY

Compiled by Gail Bird

1. Floss is sometimes called embroidery cotton or silk (English). Consists of six threads together to form a strand. Brand names are DMC, JP Coats, Anchor, Weeks Dye Works, Gentle Arts.

2. Fringe is created by cutting open very long loops of thread.

3. Gauges are plastic sleeves that slide onto the needle shaft and regulate the size of the loop or the height of the pile.

4. Igolochkoy™ is the Russian word meaning "with a little needle," a technique and a brand of tools.

5. Overstitching is the result of putting the *rows* of stitches too close together, which distorts the fabric and pile. Correct stitching results when you take tiny stitches forward and leave a space between the rows of stitches. The space is about equal to the thickness of the shaft of the needle.

6. Pile consists of the loops that the needle makes, usually on the front side of the design.

7. Punch needle is a hollow tool consisting of three parts: handle, shaft, and gauge. The shaft has a long point with an eye (back) and a bevel (front).

8. Reverse stitching refers to the flat stitch that results from punching from the pile side of the fabric (the "good" side) to form a flat line on the pile side. This requires a longer loop in order to be more stable.

9. Scratch (or drag) is the needle movement after it is punched down, when the needle comes back out of the fabric but stays on the fabric surface as it travels forward to the next downward punch. This allows for consistent and even loops on the front side.

10. Sculpt means cutting off the loops at various levels to form uneven or rounded shapes.

11. Shear means to cut off the loops at a single level (like cutting grass). A velvet texture is the result.

12. Stitch refers to the distance the needle scratches between consecutive punches. It should always be very small and even—and should be flat and it should snug into the fabric surface.

13. Tag is the last of the thread when punching one length of thread. It will usually end up on the loop side and should be cut off even with the loops.

14. Woven refers to cloth that has been made on a loom. It has a warp (the selvage edge of a fabric), and a weft (both are stable threads), and a bias that stretches.